HOW TO CHOOSE A PSYCHOTHERAPIST

HOW TO CHOOSE
A PSYCHOTHERAPIST

HOW TO CHOOSE A PSYCHOTHERAPIST

Text by

Neville Symington

Cartoons by

Joan Symington

Edited by

Andrew Symington

Conceived by

David Symington

First published in 2003 by
H. Karnac (Books) Ltd.
6 Pembroke Buildings, London NW10 6RE

Reprinted 2003

British Library Cataloguing in Publication Data

A C.I.P. for this book is available from the British Library

ISBN 1 85575 289 1

Edited, designed, and produced by The Studio Publishing Services Ltd, Exeter EX4 8JN

Printed in Great Britain

10 9 8 7 6 5 4 3 2

www.karnacbooks.com

CONTENTS

Introduction: the psychotherapy explosion 1

CHAPTER ONE
The purpose of psychotherapy 3

CHAPTER TWO
How does therapy work? 13

CHAPTER THREE
Therapeutic tasks 19

CHAPTER FOUR
Why therapy fails 25

CHAPTER FIVE
The inadequate therapist 33

CHAPTER SIX
Defining the good therapist 45

GLOSSARY 59

BIBLIOGRAPHY 61

Introduction: the psychotherapy explosion

There has been an amazing growth in the psychotherapy industry in the last fifteen years. In the Western world psychotherapy has increased fourfold. Psychotherapy diplomas have mushroomed in the universities and Chairs in psychotherapy have been created in many of them. Outside the universities psychotherapy training courses have multiplied.

Moreover, whenever there is a natural disaster the victims are offered counselling. Counselling courses abound both in the universities and in institutions organized to run such courses. Such a huge increase in psychotherapy and counselling is in answer to a need. The natural agencies for alleviating human distress, like the churches and the numerous charities which they spawned, are no longer part of the social structure for the majority, but the need for healing of emotional distress remains. The answer to that call is all around us in the ever-growing crowd of psychotherapists and counsellors.

Inevitably the standards of practice are often sacrificed in favour of answering the needs of the market. Training courses are nearly always part-time. Frequently even those who are running them are themselves poorly trained, while those who join such courses often believe that goodheartedness and concern for one's neighbour are sufficient ingredients to make a good psychotherapist.

However, since I have been professionally involved in the world of psychotherapy I have heard numerous cases where psychotherapy has been going on with a particular patient for months and years and, as far as I have been able to determine, no change has occurred at all. A passivity sets in and sessions go on and on but no change occurs. It is not uncommon to hear of people who have visited a psychotherapist for as long as ten years with no visible result.

This little book is written for patients. It is a challenge to action. Do not be satisfied with a malingering treatment. Gird your loins and challenge your therapist and be prepared to go to a new one. It is worth going to the trouble of finding the right person. Psychotherapy is a long and expensive process so ensure that you make it effective. It is your responsibility to find the right person. This book is a guide to help you in that search.

CHAPTER ONE

The purpose of psychotherapy

The aim of psychotherapy is to cure sickness of the mind. But what is sickness of the mind? What are its causes and symptoms? How does it come to be? What does it feel like to be mentally ill? These questions when applied to physical sickness are easier to answer.

Physical sickness is felt as a pain, be it a sting or an ache or a feeling of queasiness and the doctor cures the sickness by administering an appropriate drug. Physical sickness handicaps the patient in some way and stops the body from performing one of its functions properly. A touch of rheumatism might restrict the neck from turning, a bad dose of athlete's foot might stop the patient from walking or make it painful to do so. However, very often the body might not be functioning to its full potential although the person feels no specific pain. A man may slip into the comfortable habit of enjoying three hearty meals a day and avoid physical exertion whenever he can. He is likely then to grow fat. He may for many months not notice any problem and will feel quite comfortable with his portly self. However when it happens that the elevator in his office stops working and some extraordinary physical exertion is required he may then suddenly become aware of how inadequate his body has become. Of course he may be lucky and never need to depart from his routine and place undue strain on his body.

There are also much more serious physical conditions like pneumonia or cancer that require specialist knowledge for their treatment. An ordinary layman may know the remedy for the less serious conditions, but not for these bodily catastrophes. In these cases someone with knowledge is needed.

Mental illness can also be a serious handicap. Sometimes it may be something quite mild and a friend or concerned neighbour may be able to suggest a remedy that will help, but there are cases where something much more serious occurs. A patient may be suddenly overcome by a deep and terrifying sadness which has no apparent cause. It may be a sadness that is so intense that it assaults the personality. The person finds he cannot think properly, cannot remember things or finds that he has forgotten how to drive. Or it may be that he finds everyone around him being horrible to him. Something like an explosion has gone off inside him and all he

knows is the effects of it. The afflicted person finds he can no longer function like he used to.

The mind like the body has many duties to perform and it can be affected in many different ways. So what duties does the mind perform?

(1) It reasons logically and coherently arranges thoughts.
(2) It creates through the use of the imagination.
(3) It stores experiences in memory.
(4) It is the storehouse of our emotions: love, guilt, hatred, envy, etc. Mental illness can affect any of the above functions. Mental illness is most apparent and obvious to onlookers when it affects the first of these functions. When someone does not appear to think logically we then make comments like, "he must be crackers!"

However if someone isn't functioning to their full creative

KEEP AWAY FROM HER OR YOU MIGHT CATCH SOMETHING

capacity or if they are emotionally disturbed, it is much more difficult to detect. Unless you know someone intimately, you would not know whether they are functioning to their full creative potential or not. Emotionally too, a person may seem to be functioning well. He may have a harmonious marriage and family. But like our fat man who did not discover what his body lacked until forced to use the stairs, a marriage or a family may only be held together while the winds are favourable. It is not until they face serious trials that fatal flaws are discovered. Such weaknesses, of course may never be discovered and the family or the marriage may continue undisturbed until death. When a mental illness affects a person's emotional life or creativity, people may know it but they won't think of it as a disease. An artist's work deteriorates and people may not notice.

Everyone knows someone who is incredibly shy or is unbearably pompous, but such people are not seen as suffering from a disease like a person who is not able to reason. Rather we just see them as abnormalities in the person's character. Usually we would say that if someone is shy that is simply how they are and nothing can be done about it. To the therapist, though, such peculiarities of character are signs of mental disorder which can be cured. Some people may not worry about these handicaps in their character until they seriously interfere with their functioning. A man is fired from his job, a woman loses all her confidence when a relationship breaks up and they turn then to a psychotherapist for help.

A breakdown has occurred and people do not notice—they may even, if the person is an artist, think it is an artistic breakthrough, not a breakdown.

THIS IS A REAL BREAKTHROUGH ...

As far as society is concerned, mental illness is only a problem when it threatens social harmony. Most annoying to society is when the first function of the mind—the inability to think clearly—occurs. Such mental confusion renders people agitated and worried. Society requires people to do their jobs efficiently. From this perspective it does not matter if, for example, an office worker in a government department is not functioning to his full creative capacity so long as he is doing his job. Society regards him as a nuisance, however, when his frustration starts to impair his capacity to work.

In Australia there was a recent example of this. A judge was failing to process his cases because of depression. People were waiting for three or four years for their case to come before him in the courts. Likewise, a marriage which functions but lacks passion or real understanding between the husband and wife, is of no concern to the wider society as long as the man and the woman continue to perform their respective roles adequately. It is only

when the marriage breaks down and the man and woman become irascible and depressed and start to perform less well that it becomes a problem, not only to them but to others.

Most mental treatment is a loyal servant of Society and aims to cure behaviour which disrupts social stability. It might prescribe sedatives to the frustrated office workers and aphrodisiacs to the husband and wife. If that returns them to doing their normal jobs again, Society is satisfied.

Therapy, on the other hand, is concerned with actually treating the cause of the mental disorder. Therapy goes beyond what society demands of it. To use our analogy of the fat man, instead of

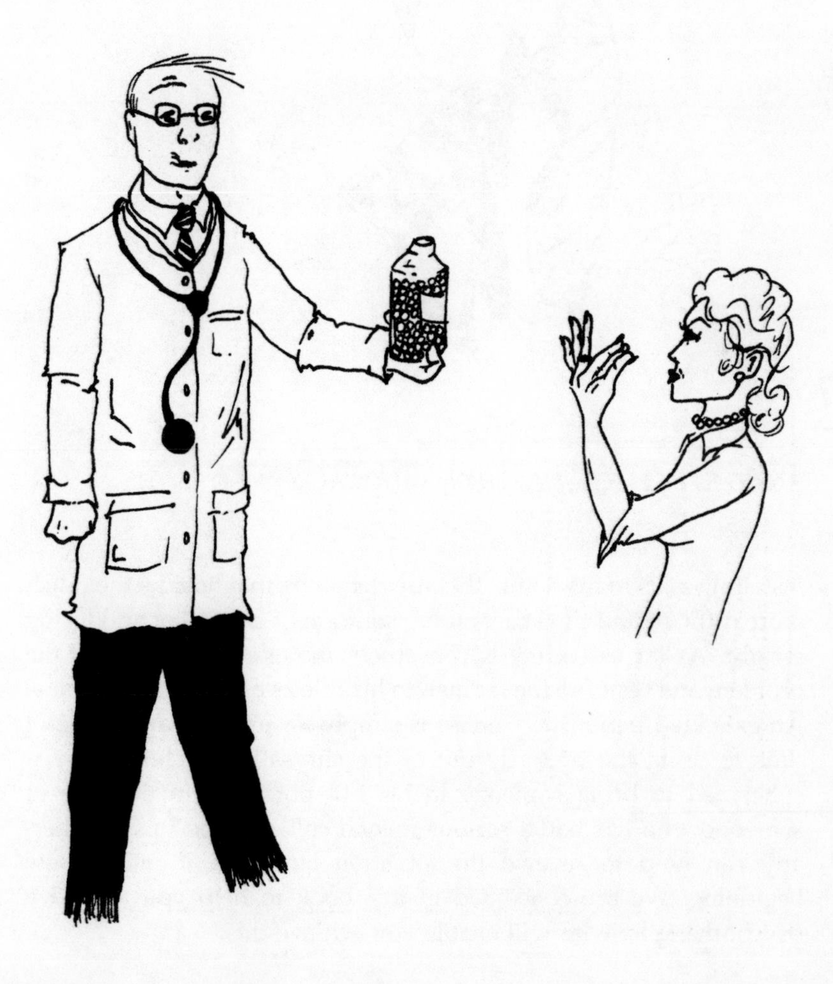

BUTTERFLY EMERGING FROM CHRYSALIS

installing a lift in his home, therapy demands that he take the much more difficult and time consuming solution of exercising and losing weight. As far as society is concerned, though, the lift solved the problem and restored the fat man to his role as a cog in the machine. An extended period of exercise is simply an unnecessary waste of time to bring the butterfly out of the chrysalis. Psychotherapy is concerned to bring someone to his full potential. In the case of someone who has had a serious mental collapse good psychotherapy can help to reverse the situation and turn it into a new beginning. We are concerned in this book to help you to find a psychotherapist who will enable you achieve this.

Summary

Mental illness, whether mild or more serious may affect a person's ability to function adequately. They may be unable to think coherently, to remember clearly, to use their imagination, or to function well emotionally. The purpose of psychotherapy is not only to rectify these problems but also to allow a person to utilize their full potential.

CHAPTER TWO

How does therapy work?

The clinician heals through talking to the patient. This is called psychotherapy. Therapy of this sort holds up a mirror to the soul of the patient. The patient changes as soon as he understands himself. The therapist's job is to give birth to understanding.

Getting to know yourself is painful. A person may think that he is a devout Christian and suddenly finds that he is a scoundrel. This is a shock to the system and it takes an experienced psychotherapist to manage the person's confusion and difficulty.

When the patient gets a glimpse of himself as a scoundrel he then tries to obliterate this troubling portrait. A therapist needs to be firm but caring to help the patient manage this alarming new insight. The therapist also needs to be emotionally robust to be able to do this properly. He becomes the messenger of bad news and the patient hates the messenger and wishes to kill him.

One of the most important qualities for a psychotherapist to possess is emotional robustness. A psychotherapist needs to be able to manage being hated, accused and insulted. A patient in a critical state needs to be able to do this and to know that she is not going to be attacked in return.

THE PATIENT GETS A GLIMPSE OF HIMSELF AS A SCOUNDREL

The therapist gauges the patient's mental state by observing the nature of her relationship with others. This more than anything else tells the therapist the patient's state of mental health. If the patient is incapable of love, if she allows herself to be trampled over, if she has no concern for others' feelings then there is a mental disorder. The therapy itself can be seen as a sample of how she behaves towards other people in her life. The patient engages in dialogue with the therapist and forges a bond with him. The only relationship that the therapist knows about first hand is the patient's way of connecting with him. The therapist may find that the patient imagines him to be quite unlike what he really is. Now the therapist has some real stuff to grapple with. The therapist observes carefully how the patient reacts with and treats him and, by extension, gains insight into the distortions of the patient's mental functioning and how this affects others in the patient's life.

PATIENT SHOOTS THE THERAPIST AS THE MESSENGER OF BAD NEWS

WHEN THE PATIENT BECOMES AWARE OF HOW MADLY HE IS BEHAVING HE WANTS TO SMASH HIS BRAIN

This would be fraught with difficulty if the therapist did not have a good understanding of himself. If the therapist were the sort of person who tends to be treated very badly by people and to be walked over, he would start diagnosing all his patients as being very cruel and thoughtless. It is for this reason that an essential ingredient of the therapist's training is to go through therapy himself. It is a perfectly valid question therefore to ask a therapist whether he has had therapy himself. If your problem is that you always get into trouble with close emotional relationships then you would not want to find yourself with a therapist who had exactly the same problem. On the other hand if you went to a therapist who had had that problem and had resolved it in his own therapy it gives him a special personal insight into that particular difficulty. This is why some therapists are much better with certain kinds of patient than with others. If things are not going well it is perfectly valid for you to say you would like a second opinion. If the therapist is unhappy about that then it is a sign that he is not to be trusted further.

Once the therapist knows himself well he can disentangle and separate clearly the patient's mind from his own. The central goal of the therapist is to offer the patient self-knowledge. The quality of therapists who practise in this way varies considerably. An innocent observer would be rightly suspicious of paying someone simply to talk to them and give them nothing tangible. There is a great deal of difference between therapists who do no more than talk (who are unfortunately in the great majority) and those who truly endeavour to heal.

Summary

Therapy works by a patient gaining self-knowledge through understanding. This understanding is acquired within the context of a professional relationship with the therapist. The process can be emotionally painful and a therapist must not only have a good understanding of himself, but also be emotionally strong and able to withstand the patient's anger. A well-trained therapist will have completed therapy himself.

BLA, BLA, BLA...
I'M PAYING SO I CAN TALK...

CHAPTER THREE

Therapeutic tasks

I once met a woman whose mother, father, and sister were shot in front of her eyes; she was ten years old at the time. When I tell you that she was neurotic your justified reply will be, "I am not surprised. The only thing that amazes me is that she has any sanity at all. I should have thought she would be in the chronic ward of a mental hospital."

I have heard cases that have made me want to curse the gods that produced such an appalling species on this planet. And when the victims of these appalling events come for help what is the therapist to do? What is her task? She cannot change the events, she cannot unroll the cinema of life and re-play it so that this shivering ten year old sees her parents saved from disaster. There is only one thing the therapist can do and that is to help the patient strengthen her mind so she can manage the disaster. That is the therapist's task. The therapist who keeps that in mind as his prime aim will be a good therapist; the one who forgets it will fail his patients. How does the therapist achieve this objective? I want to tell you a story that gives us some clue.

A woman living in India lost her new-born child. In great distress she went to a holy man and asked him if he could give back to her the life of her child. He understood her great grief and told her to bring him five mustard seeds given to her by a family that had suffered no disaster and he would then grant her wish. The distressed woman went from house to house but could not find one which was free of tragedy. She realized the significance of what the holy man had said to her and became mentally able to bear the disaster that had befallen her.

This man was a therapist by definition as he helped to strengthen her mind in the face of disaster. How did he achieve his task? Let us take the elements one by one.

Empathy

The first essential is that he understood her distress. How? It can only be that he had suffered a crisis in his own life and come to terms with it mentally. He has not lost a newborn child, but through having suffered disaster himself and assimilated it into his mind he has the capacity to understand the distress of another. The particular distress will be different, but there is enough commonality of suffering for him naturally to have empathy for her. He has within him the experience necessary and sufficient reflection upon it to be able to embrace her suffering emotionally. To be able to do this he has not only to have suffered a crisis but also to have assimilated it into his mind. This process of assimilating traumas into our mental life is why a therapist attends therapy sessions himself as part of his training. If he has achieved this he will be understanding of his patient and not condemning. If he does not do this then he will be unable to have sympathy for his own patients. The woman who lost her child came to hold the distress of it within her own soul. One could be sure that she would in turn become sympathetic towards others in their distress.

When you are looking for a therapist it is up to you to decide whether you think that this therapist has suffered enough and assimilated the tragedies of life sufficiently to be able to help you. If your "gut feeling" is that he cannot help you then trust that feeling and seek someone else. People often have that "gut feeling" but then reject it, letting their surface feelings rule the day. When you go to a therapist you spend a great deal of time, money, and effort so disregarding that deeper feeling can cost you dearly, not only in money and time, but in terms of your own fulfillment and happiness.

Knowledge of the mind

The holy man knew that this woman was trying to solve her distress by resorting to magic and god-like thinking. He knew that her mental health would only be restored when she had renounced this magical belief. From her request to him he was able to diagnose that she believed in magic. He knew that she would have to renounce this belief if she was to become mentally healthy again.

So a therapist can only help his patient if he has knowledge of the mind. In this case the holy man understood the magical processes of the mind and their inability to solve a person's problems. He had an understanding of the need for sad events to be received slowly but surely into the fabric of the mind. Is there any way in which the patient can know whether the therapist has this knowledge? There are plenty of therapists who know nothing about the mind and its processes. It is certain that it takes a long time to come to such an understanding. It is unlikely that a therapist who is very young would have this knowledge. It is not knowledge that can be gained by attendance at a few conferences or by finishing a part-time training course in psychotherapy. This in no way means that it is possessed by an older person or that someone who has done a full-time rigorous course is necessarily a well-equipped therapist. So when you are looking for a therapist you need to look for signs of this knowledge.

First sign

In the first interview did the therapist help you understand something which you had not understood before? When the interview is over, ask yourself the question, "Do I understand something now which I did not understand before?" In the above story it is clear that the holy man had understood what was impeding the woman's mind from finding recovery. If the answer is "no" then you should try someone else.

Second sign

Subsequent to the interview did you experience any change in your mood, your feelings or your way of responding to people? If not then the interview has had no impact upon you and you would do better to find another therapist. This does not mean that you necessarily feel better, but rather than you note a change in either your inner mood or a change in your outer behaviour. In the story, the woman had a realization and a change of attitude after her encounter with the holy man. However, it is no good going to visit a therapist in a state of mind that is too suspicious. You need to be quite free in your communication with him. This will enable him to understand what is handicapping your mind. Only then can you apply these two criteria. If on both signs you get a negative then I would definitely choose another therapist.

What you want is a therapist who has knowledge and understanding. Do not be deceived by "niceness". This is not a quality that is important. If you are easily seduced by people being nice to you then be particularly careful because you may choose a therapist who will be nice, but no help to you at all.

Ego-Centricity

One aspect of this woman's problem was her ego-centricity which the holy man realized. By telling her to go around and find a home in which there had been no tragedy he was trying to bring her to the realization that her situation was not unique, that she was part of the human family. To become fully conscious that your own suffering is shared by others is a source of considerable healing. The holy man understood this because he had been on a similar journey himself.

Interpretation

When you go to a therapist you may want advice. If you get it then don't go to him! If he says something that shows he understands what you are anxious about then you have probably found the right person for you. When what the therapist has said shows he understands why you are anxious or troubled he has made what is called an interpretation. If the therapist tries to impose a point of view on you that seems quite off the mark and continues to insist on it then go to another therapist.

If you get the sense that he has heard what you have to say then you have probably found the right person. The therapist's job is to make an interpretation. In the story the holy man's instruction becomes an interpretation. The woman understands that suffering is part of life and is everyone's lot and realizes that to believe her baby can come to life again is an understandable but fruitless wish. Her baby does not come back to life but a new emotional seed takes root in her personality. She ends by becoming a stronger and wiser person.

An interpretation confronts you with the real facts of the situation. Ask yourself afterwards whether the therapist confronted you in this

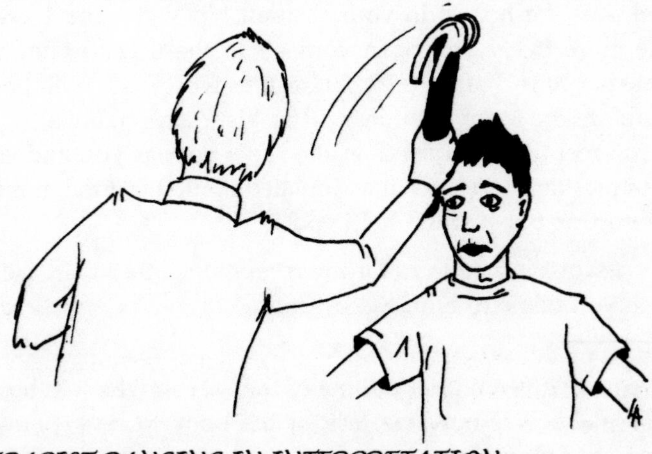

THERAPIST BANGING IN INTERPRETATION

way. If the answer is "no" then you won't make progress with this therapist. Remember that when you go for therapy you have a job that needs to be done just as when you go to the doctor or the dentist.

Summary

There are a number of shorthand rules to determine whether a therapist is going to be able to help you or not.

(1) Interpretations are the therapist's "medicine chest." Did the therapist give me some interpretations that really helped?
(2) In going into therapy you enter in a relationship with a therapist. Could you say that you have a relationship with your therapist?
(3) The therapist judges your web of relationships from his relationship with you. Have you found that your way of relating to family and friends (and enemies!) is different ?
(4) An egocentric therapist won't help his patient to find his own fulfillment.

Therefore:

(1) If the interpretations of the therapist make no sense to you the therapy is completely pointless. However you must think carefully about the interpretations. Although you may dislike an interpretation it may be very accurate.
(2) Your relationship, like all real relationships, will be one fraught with difficulties. You can expect bitter arguments and fights.
(3) You must be honest in your relationship with your therapist. The more freely you open yourself to the therapist the more realistic your "sample" relationship with him will be and therefore the more accurate will be his interpretations.
(4) If you feel the therapist is in the same boat as you and shares your problem and has not assimilated it into his mind, it may be comforting but it won't help you.

NB. A therapist has sources for interpretations other than the way in which you relate to him, e.g. dreams.

* * *

Now we have given a brief outline of the way in which a therapist plies his trade. It is now the task of the book to reveal how the therapist can fail in his endeavour.

CHAPTER FOUR

Why therapy fails

The unengaged therapist

The therapist needs to be emotionally engaged with you and your problems. The idea that the therapist needs to be living in his own detached world unaffected by what you say or do is not only false but extremely damaging. A therapist needs to be alive and vital and responsive to what is happening.

A Scottish therapist displayed a remote detachment to an infamous degree. A patient used to tell nasty and unpleasant jokes about Scotland and the Scots during sessions, but the therapist did not react to this at all. It was not that he felt something but was biding his time before speaking. He was in an insulation chamber so that he actually did not feel anything when the patient made these abusive comments. When asked how he felt about being treated in this way he said he felt nothing.

> "But how would you feel if someone spoke like that to you at a party—how would you feel then?"
> "I would be bloody angry."
> "Why weren't you angry when the patient spoke to you like that?"
> "Therapists are not supposed to be angry," he said.

SHOUTING THERAPIST

There is a shocking misconception here. There is a difference between feeling something and the way that feeling is processed. If the Scottish therapist said to his patient, "How dare you speak to me like that", it would be unhelpful.

It would be unhelpful because the therapist's job is to convert raw feeling into understanding, like a painter's job is to convert the colours on his palette into a painting. Feelings are the paints on the palette and it is the job of the therapist to convert them not into a painting but into an understanding. If he shouts at the patient in anger then he has not converted them. On the other hand, if he has no feelings then he has nothing out of which to fashion an understanding. He is like the painter who has forgotten to take his oil colours with him. He looks down at his palette and there is nothing there.

So what has happened here? The therapist has anaesthetized himself. The patient will have as much chance of being helped by such a therapist as he would if he discovered that his therapist was sound asleep. If you went to visit your doctor and you found him

THE THERAPIST WITH FEELINGS IS LIKE AN ARTIST WITH NO PAINTS

lying on the floor of his surgery dead drunk you would go to another doctor.

Are there any signs that will tell you that the therapist is in this drugged state? This is a difficult one. You do not expect him to shout at you but you do expect him to be affected by what you say and do. Can you get any sign of whether this is the case? The answer is "yes", but the sign is in yourself, not in your observation of your therapist. If the therapist is being affected by what you say and do, you will find that you change in your disposition. Moods are transmitted from one to another and so you can expect a change in your feelings but if the therapist is in the drugged state you won't. What sort of changes do you need to look for? The following are some indicators:

(1) Have you noticed any ways in which you have been able to deal with things more effectively. For example, do you find that you can manage that bully at work better than you could?

THE DRUGGED THERAPIST

(2) Have you had any "realizations" that are new to you? Have you seen your mother, father, partner, children or friends in a new light?

(3) Have you had an understanding of yourself which is quite new? It does not have to be something major but nevertheless something quite definite. A businessman noticed that he was able to negotiate a satisfactory deal more easily than he had before. Another person realized that she had a gift for friendship which she never knew she had before. You may,

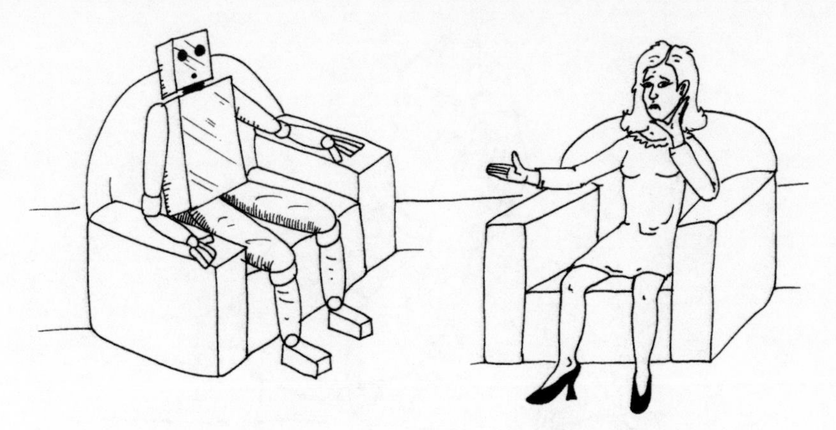

THE ROBOT THERAPIST—NO CHANGE IN THE PATIENT

for instance realize that you are capable of doing a more worthwhile job than you are doing at present.

In other words you look at yourself and see whether you have changed in a significant way. If you have then you can be assured that your therapist is not anaesthetized, because these changes will have come about through an interaction with your therapist who is alive and flourishing. If you can honestly say that you cannot see any changes in yourself then you need to be alert to the possibility that your therapist is a paralyzed automaton.

One way of getting some perspective on this is to ask yourself whether you know what kind of person your therapist is. A friend asks you "What is he like?" and if you can give a reasonable character sketch then that is a good sign that your therapist is a real person and not a robot.

The patient as Jekyll and Hyde

If the patient has bothered to come to therapy and the therapist wants to cure him, how can the process fail? A fundamental paradox needs to be explained. A patient can both want to be cured but hate changing himself and therefore do all in his power to hinder the progress of the therapy. Using the analogy of the fat man, the paradox can be understood. The fat man recognizes that there is something wrong with him when he cannot ascend the stairs as he

once was able to. The solution, exercise and eating fewer cup-cakes, may be just as hateful to him as his lack of fitness.

The mentally ill patient may suffer from many symptoms he loathes. He may find himself lonely and cast out by his colleagues. The cause of that will most likely be very deep-seated, not something trivial. The thought that he may have to change something very fundamental, is often devastating. A patient will often say something like, "but this shyness is so much part of me I cannot imagine living without it". An unhealthy mental attitude can be like a family member someone is attached to.

So you must expect the therapist to combat that hatred of change in you. So if you feel angry and hateful then that may be a good sign—that you have a therapist who is combating some deeply ingrained habit in you that is like a cancer which devours your life. The challenge for the therapist is to stick to his guns and not be brow-beaten by you. You may feel angry at the time when your therapist has challenged a cherished habit, but later you will be glad because you can see some good effects coming your way.

You have both a co-operative side in you and a side that wants to sabotage the process. As many therapists are not aware of this sabotaging side be suspicious if the therapist seems to accept all that you say and does not challenge anything. Remember that you have gone for therapy because something is not working out properly in your life. There is something in you then that is against your own best interests. You want a therapist who is able to detect this and get your co-operation against it. You need to feel yourself coming up against the therapist, feel that after a session with him you have had a real encounter. A woman went to see a therapist and after the interview wiped her brow with exhaustion. All her emotions had been engaged during the interview. You want someone who is both receptive to what you have to say but who will also give you something from himself.

Also think to yourself, "Despite your best efforts at trying to hide your symptoms, has the therapist uncovered some of your areas of shame? Do you feel exposed in the face of the therapist. If you feel this then it is likely that the therapist is doing a good job. You may have become expert at hiding your difficulties and you may be able to confound your therapist. Speak to yourself honestly and ask yourself whether you have pulled the wool over your therapists' eyes. If you have then you need someone sharper, better able to "see through you".

THE SHARP THERAPIST—THE THERAPIST YOU WANT

Summary

Therapy fails because:

(1) YOU are resisting mental change. Therapy isn't meant to be easy. If you want your therapy to be successful you must be prepared to accept very unpalatable truths about yourself. Ask yourself if your therapist has delivered into your bosom uncomfortable truths. If you have not been challenged about the way you have conducted your life so far then it is time to think of changing to another therapist.

(2) The THERAPIST isn't firm enough or, worse still, isn't aware that you are sabotaging the process. You can't be expected to be a saint so the therapist may need to evoke what is strong in you and challenge any wimpishness. Consider whether your therapist is being too soft with you. What you need in a psychotherapist is someone who will take your side against the traitor inside you.

CHAPTER FIVE

The inadequate therapist

The seductive therapist

Very many psychotherapists are guilty of collaborating with the patient against others in his life. I call such therapists seductive therapists. Such therapists do not see collusion with their patient as a fault. Far from it. They actually see it as their role to be a support to the patient. Their motives are laudable, but the simple facts are that if you want mental change and cure to occur you must go to a therapist who challenges you.

There was a famous psychologist called Wolfgang Kohler who put a banana just out of reach of Nueva, a chimpanzee, who was in a cage. Nueva whimpered and pleaded with Wolfgang to give her the banana but he did not do so. Then she sulked and pouted and finally climbed up a tree and sat thinking. There was a stick in the cage and suddenly she leapt down from the tree and picked up the stick and by using it managed to pull the banana within reach and then she grabbed it with her hand and ate it contentedly. Now if Wolfgang had given into her pleading and handed her the banana Nueva would not have discovered that she could herself solve the problem. Through acting in the way he did Nueva found the

solution through her own thinking capacities. So make sure that your therapist does not give into your pleadings for her to do the job for you. If you have repeated evidence that she does then go to someone else.

A very common problem in today's society is the break-up of families and divorce. I believe that the psychotherapist often plays a great part in this. The seductive psychotherapist will encourage his patient to express anger against his spouse during sessions and be a support to him. The reason often given for such behaviour is that it is better to have the emotions out in the open. A divorce will often be described as inevitable and that the therapist should support one party through that traumatic time. You may decide to separate from your partner but whether you do or not the decision is yours. The therapist's job is to help you do battle with those things inside you that obscure your vision, obscure your understanding, obscure your perception.

Picking the seductive therapist

It is very difficult to pick a seductive therapist because:

(1) Being seductive he will go out of his way to appear concerned and friendly. If you are in a bad state that will be a great comfort.

(2) What the therapist does not do rather than what he actually does do is where the problem lies. He will use tactics like the mirroring tactic mentioned later which do nothing, but are not obviously harmful and are difficult to detect.

How do you determine if your therapist is being seductive?

(1) A feeling of emptiness at the end of sessions.
(2) You may notice that you are never annoyed, frustrated or angry during sessions. Ironically, that is a bad sign.
(3) Remember feeling relaxed is NOT the goal. You don't need to pay someone to relax. Just drink a glass of brandy and find the softest armchair in your house.

The mirroring psychotherapist

Patient, "I feel really low and full of despair today."
Therapist, "I can see you're depressed and you feel like giving up."

Here the therapist has mirrored back what the patient has just said to him. This procedure is extremely common but what does it achieve? Does it accomplish anything? All the therapist is doing is filling the room with words. It is the therapist's mind and your mind in interaction that brings about mental change.

The therapist, as I keep stressing, must be thinking and questioning your words and seeking to understand the meaning behind them. When the patient says he's depressed the therapist should be wondering why, with his mind probing for understanding. Remember that healing will come to you through your mind and his mind reaching mutual understanding. So if you find your therapist repeating what you have said then his mind is not engaging in the right place. If you find that your therapist is repeating what you have just said then consider going to someone else. This type of behaviour on the part of the therapist is almost worse than out-and-out abusive behaviour because at least with the latter the failure on the part of the therapist is obvious whereas you may not notice when he is just benignly holding up a mirror to what you are saying.

How to pick the mirroring psychotherapist

(1) Are you learning about your feelings?
(2) Has a new understanding come to you?
(3) Have you been "shocked" into a quite different view of things?

If none of these seems to be true then consider that your therapist may not be helping you.

The colluding therapist

To change oneself is one of the most difficult things to do. People easily get stuck into a routine and grow comfortable in it. You may want to thrust your therapist into your own comfort zone. In other words you may be in a state of complacency that you don't want disrupted, so although you may not realize it, you draw your therapist into harmony with your state. This will not help you at all. If you think that you are doing this and it has not been challenged, then have serious doubts about your therapist. To change requires emotional exertion. The most difficult thing about changing, though, is that it inevitably means an acknowledgment that the way that you have been living up to that point has been inadequate. The sense of wasted time is terrifically painful especially when you realize that you can never have that time back again. Ideally you would like your therapist to tell you that everything is okay. Tragically there are too many therapists ready to collude with this powerful desire of yours.

Therapists who collude with any complacency in your present state miss the fact that you are on a journey, trying to reach somewhere. All patients come to the therapist feeling they are failing in some way and that there is something unsatisfactory

MAGICIAN THERAPIST

about their life. Although it may provide temporary comfort to hear that they are just fine as they are, yet at a deeper level they want to hear the opposite. As with any profession, psychotherapists develop a certain mystique and aura. The pronouncements of a therapist can acquire oracular dimensions so that when you have some inner unease about how things are for you within, this can be silenced by the voice of a therapist from on high.

Like the oracles of antiquity most therapists tell the seeker of the truth just what they want to hear. While it may please the patient to be led to believe he is a good and loving husband, it will make the divorce even more painful. G. K. Chesterton was more correct than he realized when he said that psychotherapy is confession without absolution—the therapist should quickly disillusion you of the idea that you are going to get absolution from him. What a lovely feeling to have a therapist who is a magician but the end result will be disappointment.

One psychiatrist told me how he had assured his patient that she was not clinically mad. That is a form absolution. Consider this little piece of dialogue between a therapist and his supervisor (a more experienced senior therapist).

> *Therapist*: We have talked about that. I have given her much of my psychiatric experience and stated to her that there is nothing that I can see clinically to indicate that she is going the way of her mother (who had been in a mental asylum).
>
> *Supervisor*: I should be very wary of saying that sort of thing to her. The reason is that I suspect that she stimulates that response in you, a comforting response. When you say that to her, you soothe her. You say it because she is fearfully worried that she is going to go mad like her mother. The question to address is why she believes that she is going to follow in her mother's footsteps.
>
> *Therapist*: Well no, I can't say that she was anxious about it.
>
> *Supervisor*: I don't think you'd have said it unless she was anxious. Your remark was to soothe away the fearful thought that she might go mad like her mother. I think it's a very important therapeutic principle that you allow that thought to be. I do not mean that you just let her suffer. That would be heartless but that rather than make it disappear through your magic pronouncement you try to understand what it is that is producing this panic in her.

THERAPIST WASHING AWAY ALL PROBLEMS

The fundamental thing the therapist must understand is, as I described earlier, that the patient has a side which seeks to sabotage the psychotherapeutic process. The destructive force is the one which sees the therapist as a magician and is thirsty for his water of ablution.

The constructive side of your personality, however, finds its origins in that unease that brought you to your therapist in the first place. That constructive side in you hopes that the therapist will support you in finding the source of the unease, your desire to find a solution against that other side of you that looks for a magical recipe.

A therapist from Berlin was seeing a female patient who was very disturbed. So disturbed was this patient that she came for treatment six days a week for one hour. The therapist began to notice a slight improvement in the symptoms being shown by the patient. One morning the therapist received a telephone call from the woman.

"I want to take a week's holiday in Saarbrücken. I'm feeling better and I think I can manage it. Do you think it's okay if I don't come for my sessions next week?" said the patient.

The therapist replied, "That's fine". The conversation ended thus. As soon as she put down the receiver, though, the woman took a letter opener and stabbed herself. Fortunately she just missed her heart and recovered in hospital.

On the surface this woman was asking her therapist whether she could go for a week without seeing him. In fact, though, she was trying to ascertain whether (as she saw it) the therapist really cared for her. If the therapist had really cared for her (she thinks) he would surely not have allowed her to be away from him for a week. She therefore took a knife to herself. This may seem an extraordinary and fantastic case but such events are much more common than you might think. It illustrates very graphically the tragic consequences that can spring from a therapist taking his patient too literally and misreading the patient's true meaning. It also illustrates the difficulties inherent in the relationship between therapist and patient which is on the one hand very formal and professional but also very intimate. It shows that the emotional temperature between therapist and patient is very high.

The patient is sometimes a natural dissimulator. This woman, though highly disturbed, could hardly have asked the therapist outright whether he cared for her. She would have known that the therapist would have answered in the affirmative whatever his true feelings. So she has to spin a web of deceit in which to catch a negative response from the unsuspecting therapist. The therapist should have picked non-verbal cues from the sessions immediately before the phone call or even during the phone call which would have told him that all was far from well. It seems almost fantastic that a woman could be within minutes of killing herself and for her to show absolutely no signs of it. The therapist should be wary of getting caught up in extraneous surface details of the patient's story.

It is worth thinking a bit more about this patient's problem. She was focused upon the therapist's attitude towards her but her own attitude was violently self-destructive. It was so self-destructive that she could hardly bear to look at it. Instead she used all her psychic energy in trying to detect the minutest sign of uncaringness in him.

THERAPIST DETECTING THE INNER CANCER

What is certain in this case is that the patient had no care for herself. The therapist had not uncovered this malignant inner cancer. The therapist's job is to detect this inner cancer and solicit the patient's collaboration in fighting against it.

If you see it really clearly you may take up the cudgels and fight against it. When Churchill said to the English people in 1940: "Blood, sweat and tears is all I have to offer you", he was not implying: "So you might as well lie down and die" but rather: "Rise up and meet the challenge".

The therapist needs to be very wary of getting caught up in the extraneous details of the patient's story. It was not the therapist's job to determine whether his patient could stay some days in Saarbrücken, but rather to ask himself, "Why the hell is she asking me this? What is the inner mental attitude that is prompting this question?" If you find that your therapist is giving you a lot of advice then go to someone else.

The therapist needs, therefore, to be aware of the sub-conscious level of much communication. If you have examples of your therapist having this awareness then you are probably with the right person. Here is a clinical example.

An incident occurred with one patient I treated which illustrates that much is communicated without the spoken word. A man was very depressed because his business was going badly, his wife was unresponsive to him and he couldn't stop himself getting drunk. He was full of self-loathing. So here he was with a very unhealthy attitude. Rather than rising up and tackling the problem he was wallowing in self-pity. On the surface it seems as if he thinks that he is worthless but the therapist noticed that he could not bear to consider that he was affected by what the therapist said or did. He was above being affected or influenced by others:

> I am the ruler of my own life. No one will ever tell me what to do. I am not like these people who always run to others for advice …

However the opposite was the truth. When the psychotherapist went away he lay at home and masturbated and did not even go to work. The therapist with much tact and care pointed out how much he was affected by what people did and how he pretended to be an isolated heroic king but in fact he crumpled as soon as someone important to him went away. The therapist was able to show him how damaging this mental attitude was. Slowly his attitude changed. His business improved and his wife became loving towards him. He had had a change of heart. Through seeing the inner cancer he had gone in search of something robust and resilient in himself. This came about because the therapy was able to tap into the creative resources in himself. So when you go to a therapist ask yourself if your attitude has changed as a result of going to the therapist? Have people begun to relate to you differently? Do people respect you more? Are you able to bear people's anger more easily? Are you more courageous? Do you love more? These are the questions you need to ask yourself. If the answer is "Yes" then you have found a good therapist but if "No" then go in search of someone else.

Summary

A therapist is inadequate when he colludes with a patient by being supportive rather than challenging. This may result in a feeling of emptiness at the end of a session or by feeling relaxed and comforted. A second form of inadequacy is when the therapist mirrors back the patient's words without understanding and questioning their meaning. Under these circumstances a patient will not gain new understanding or learn about her feelings.

CHAPTER SIX

Defining the good therapist

You may ask yourself whether it is possible to find a good therapist. This is a valid question and the whole implication of this book is that the good therapist is a rare commodity. However we also believe that it is well worth the search. It is far better to find a good therapist who may practise a long way from your place of work or where you live or may be more costly than seems possible. It is better to go once a fortnight to someone who is really right for you than to go more often to someone who may be more convenient, but who will not help you. I will go even further than this. It is better to be without a therapist than to go to someone who does not help you. In the first case you at least know that you do not have anyone and there is no pretence. In the second, you are in danger of deluding yourself.

The therapist's task is to help you change your internal environment and not be seduced away into cataloguing all the woes of the external environment. You should not be seduced into accepting a role as a victim of circumstance and of society. Nothing could be more damaging, because it is confirmation to you that the situation is out of your control. If there is something in you that leads you into trouble then there is hope because you can do

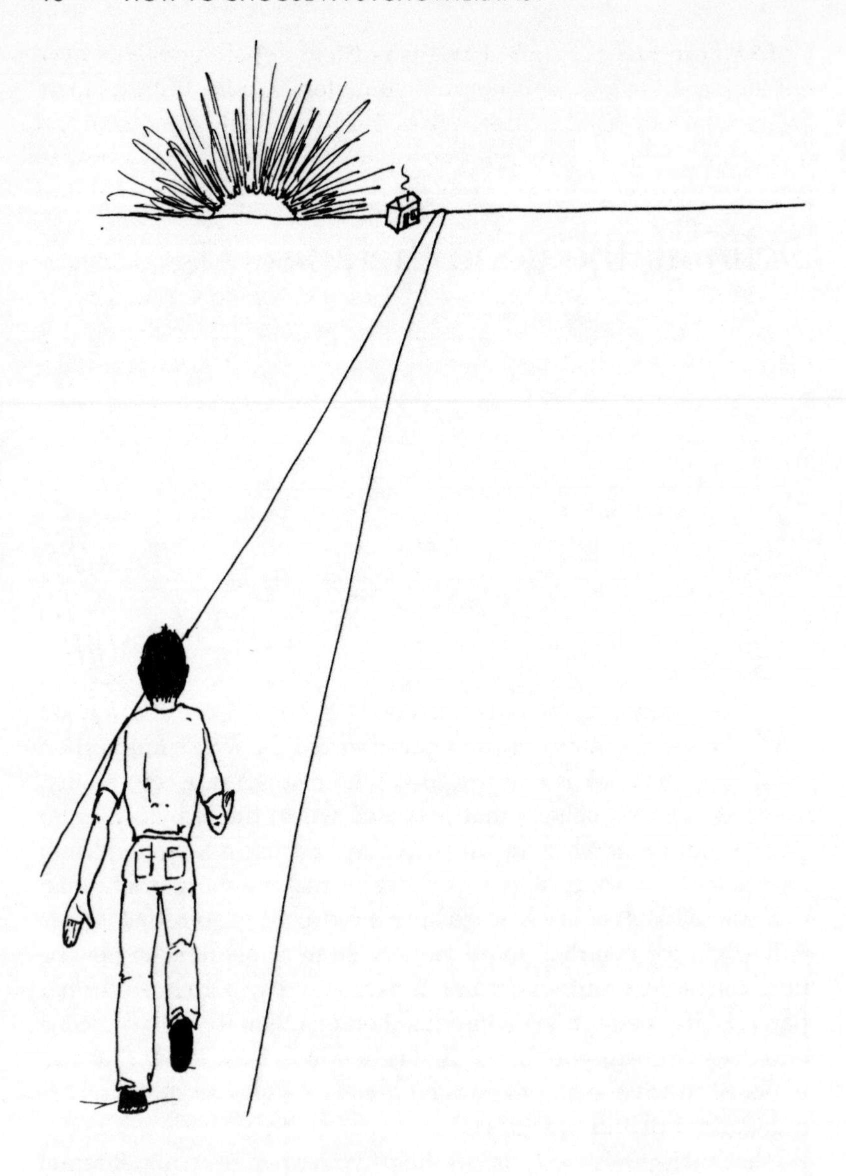

something about it. I gave the example at the beginning of chapter three of the woman who, at the age of ten, saw her parents shot before her eyes. If there is nothing she can do to repair the damage of that appalling event then she will despair. Make sure that your therapist brings you hope, not despair.

I want to make it clear that it is not that appalling events have not happened to you. It is not that your story is a lie, but that there is now a task to be addressed. When there is a great earthquake and thousands of lives are lost there is a disaster that no one can gainsay. What we want after such an event is workers who will start to re-build the destroyed city.

This is also the psychotherapist's job. The psychological damage that has been done to you by wanton events now needs to be repaired. You will have to change yourself. The psychotherapist is there to help you achieve that. He helps you re-build your house. If you say that your husband is an absolute cad you want your

therapist to be asking herself why you married such a person. However terrible your husband may have been you must have had some role in getting such a husband. If the therapist does not get you to explore that then you will find that you end up with another man just as bad or perhaps worse. Therefore, if the therapist commiserates with you, just like a friend, you should then pack up your bags and find a therapist who will really rouse your spirit.

Many people punish themselves and do so by marrying an abusive partner. The reasons why people do this are mysterious but need to be understood. Usually there is considerable guilt buried in the person and healing will only come if this is brought to the surface and changed. You want a therapist who will root out this need for punishment in yourself. If that is understood and achieved then you will have a chance of doing things better next time.

The good therapist knows that the environment affects you and that you affect your environment. The bad therapist thinks that it is a one way street when it is a two-way street. If the therapist thinks that it is all your "fault" then he cannot help you; if he thinks that it is entirely the "fault" of others he won't help you either. For example, a patient told her therapist that she was in bed with her lover when the landlord burst in and said she was not allowed to have a man there. She got up, grabbed a knife and stabbed the landlord. The landlord's way of behaving was, no doubt, boorish and clumsy but her reaction was impulsive. Her life was a litany of such actions and she was always in trouble. Her therapist only sympathized with her plight and never came to understand why she was so impulsive and whether he could do anything to help her become more thoughtful.

Another therapist condemned her patient for treating her child so negligently. The patient felt hopeless and that there was nothing in her capable of changing the course of events. So she felt condemned and the more condemned she felt the more the child became neglected. The good therapist, on the other hand, helps you to focus on your inner emotions.

What about when a child is raped and murdered? How can the grief of the parents be repaired? Can a therapist do anything? The motto is: the worse the catastrophe the harder is the work to be done. The therapist is faced with a disaster of the human spirit. Like a doctor faced with a victim of a severe car crash. The doctor never says, "There's nothing to be done". If the patient is living he does everything in his power to save the person's life. It is the same with a disaster of the human spirit. The therapist's task is to help the person re-kindle the spirit. Sadness at the loss will never disappear. Bitterness towards the perpetrators crushes the life-blood of those parents. The therapist can help to soften the bitterness. This is a task of heroic proportions but one that needs to be addressed. Those parents will not be able to take their place in the human community and live a full life unless that bitterness softens. So the therapist has a task every bit as difficult as that which confronted the surgeon when he is faced with the car crash victim.

A man felt very bitter towards an older man who had been his boss at work and whom he felt had hampered his progress. Some years later he decided to write a novel about this man and, to his surprise, he found that he felt much more kindly towards him. His inner emotional attitude had changed. In that state his attitude towards life was much improved. It is this sort of change that the good therapist needs to be helping you to achieve. Ask yourself whether your therapist has helped you to achieve such changes.

The most important attribute of the good therapist is the ability

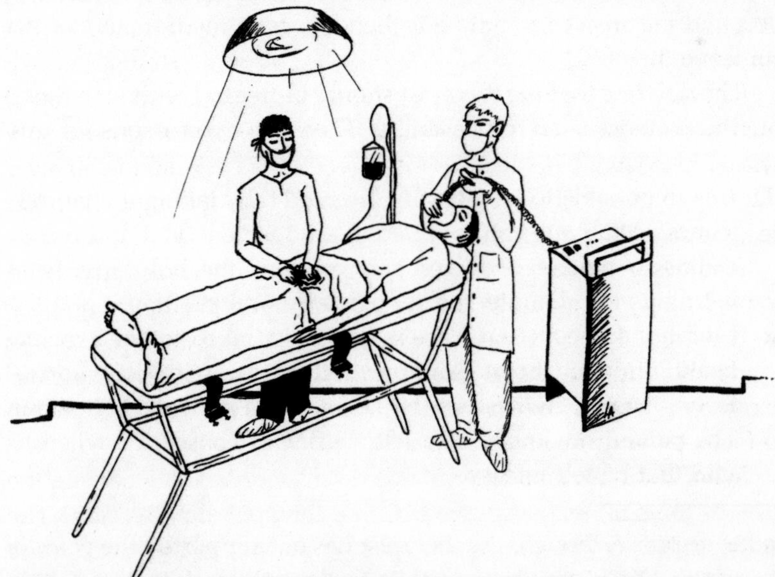

THERAPIST'S TASK AS DIFFICULT AS A SURGEON'S AFTER SOMEONE HAS HAD A CAR CRASH

to awake the constructive element in your story. You want your own creative capacities to be used to the utmost. It is these capacities in you that regenerate your life and make it meaningful again.
Make this judgment: Has my therapist helped me to rise up out of depression and face life again? If not then it may be time to choose someone else.

Therapy and morality

A man was in treatment with a therapist. While his wife was having a baby in hospital he went off with another woman for the night and after reporting this to the psychotherapist he said, "I am feeling a bit uneasy". The therapist said, "Perhaps because you feel I am going to attack you". The implication in the therapist's response is that the patient should not expect to be attacked. The therapist would claim though that he is taking a neutral stance and is not judging his patient either way. However, he is clearly over-riding (soothing) the patient's unease. Again the therapist is robbing the patient of his own source of healing within himself. If you ask yourself honestly whether your therapist is acting in this way and you find the answer is that he is then it is certainly time to look for someone different.

The doctrine that the therapist should be neutral without a moral or ethical stance is an impossibility. There are two reasons for this.

(1) It is impossible to be ethically "neutral". By taking a "neutral" stance on an issue you are making a judgement on it. If someone claims to neither condemn nor condone the holocaust he is taking a very definite and repugnant moral position.
(2) Morality and conscience are inextricably linked to one's mental health. In the above example a therapist with any normal feeling should twitch as s/he hears of the patient's behaviour. The patient obviously also felt a prick of conscience when he said that he felt uneasy.

In his response, though, the therapist has not supported the voice of conscience. Your conscience points to the source of healing within you. It tells you that you have within yourself a medicine chest. You

want a therapist who will help you to find that medicine not one who hides it from you.

The therapist's job is to support the healing treasure chest within and to avoid that side in you which says you have nothing of value within. By pretending to be neutral but really not being neutral at all, your therapist has hindered your finding the treasure that is within. Remember that the capacity for healing lies inside you.

Some therapists become moralistic and start condemning you and then you rightly feel persecuted and as soon as this happens you become paralysed. It is just as if your therapist had given you an anaesthetic that has made you unconscious.

So what would have been the ideal response when the patient said, "I feel uneasy?" The therapist could have said, for instance, "Which means that you have some qualms about what you have done". He can then hear how the patient formulates his unease. The patient is then on the verge of finding the path of healing.

A patient told his therapist that his mother was very uncaring and told her how she never came to see him in hospital after he had an appendix operation. Now the therapist should have been thinking along these lines: that this fact was such a trouble to the patient because he was so uncaring of himself. Instead the therapist

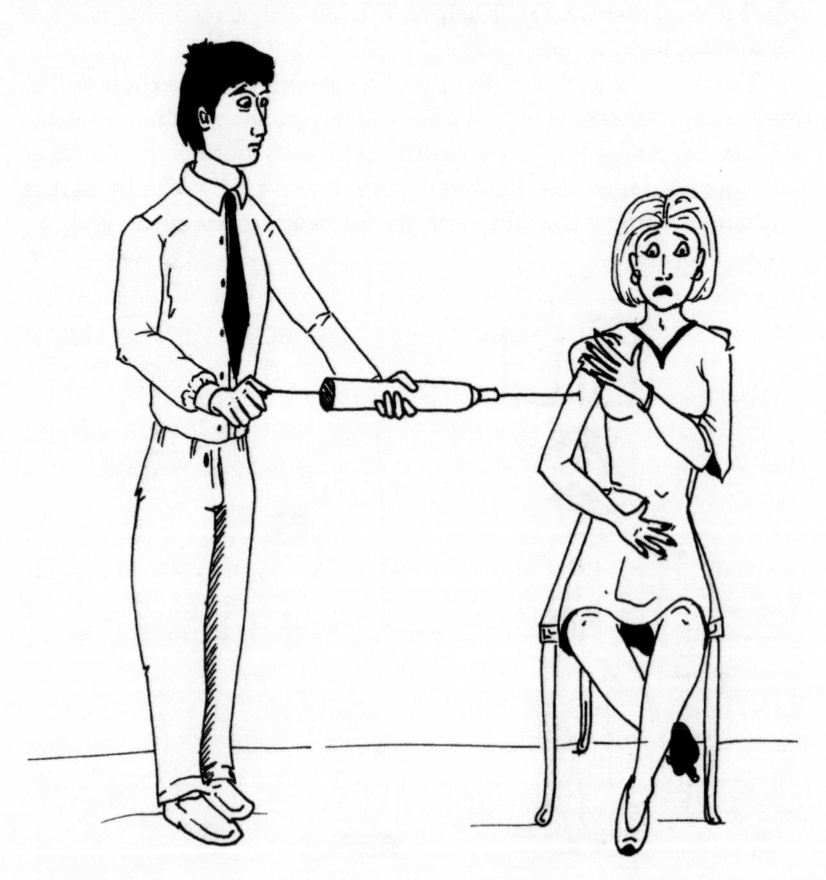

became all tied up with details about his mother. It is not that what was said about the mother was not true, but it was persecuting to the patient because it chimed with something uncaring in himself. He was always saying to himself, "Oh, I can't be bothered". What this patient needed was his therapist to sniff out this uncaring figure in himself and to rally his support against something so self-damaging.

A very interesting fact emerged with this young man. He did change therapist. The new therapist put him in touch with this uncaring attitude that he had towards himself and then one day the patient said this, "You know a very strange thing happened to me last night. I was about to go to sleep and I was thinking about that time when I was in hospital having my appendix out when I remembered very clearly that my mother *did* visit me just after I came around from the anaesthetic".

So the idea that his mother had not visited him or cared for him was a delusion and the first therapist had supported the delusion but the second allowed it to surface and find the real criminal: his own uncaring inner mother.

A successful treatment separates delusion from reality. It is very

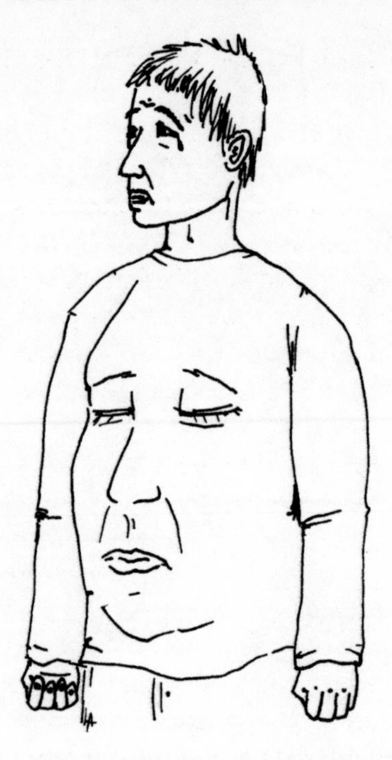

UNCARING INTERNAL MOTHER

common for a delusion to be shared by many people. I came across a case once where a young man said his father did not care about him and the man's mother echoed his complaint. There was a file on this man and a whole social work department believed that this young man's father did not care about him. It turned out however that the father cared very tenderly for the young man but the young man did not realize it and a whole social work team had been scooped into his belief.

The more you are alienated from the source of healing in yourself, the more you are victim of delusions. The reasons that the delusion surfaced in this case was that the second therapist focused upon what was uncaring inside the patient. It can happen the other way round as well. You may delude yourself that your mother is extremely caring but then memories may come back that show this to be untrue. A woman had persuaded herself that her husband was a caring man when a lot of evidence stared her in the face that he was not. Again, however, she came to this through her own understanding, helped by her therapist focusing on what was damaging her within.

This man who believed his mother did not visit him in hospital was living in a solipsistic world. When he gets into touch with his own inner uncaringness he then gets in touch with something true about his mother that he had totally wiped out of his memory. Something else is relevant: he liked to think of himself as not needing people; that he was not affected by others. If your therapy is working you will be affected by your therapist a great deal. What she says and even more, what she does, will have repercussions in your life. If this is not the case then the therapy has no hope of being effective. If you were in good management of your life you would not need to see a therapist at all. It is because you are blown this way and that by the winds of chance that you have put your faith in a therapist whom you hope will help you to become manager of your own life.

If you think that your therapist is unaware of the effect she is having on you then seriously think of changing. One day your therapist may be late. She apologises. You are affected by it. You may not want to reveal that you are but if you have clear evidence that your therapist does not realize how affected you are then it is time to change to someone else.

The most important quality in a therapist is her own self-knowledge. Her own experience of therapy should have given her knowledge of how she was affected when having treatment herself. Even if you know that your therapist had had therapy herself but she still shows a lack of understanding of how affected you are by what she does, then think seriously about going to someone else.

> A patient went to a therapist and noticed that when she spoke of something distressing he started wringing his hands and her gut feeling was that he was anxious and she decided to go to someone else. With the new person she immediately found that her pain was received and understood. Following her gut feeling was absolutely right in this case.

Trust your gut feeling. I don't mean by this your passing annoyance or happiness but a deeper inner conviction. This is what has to be trusted. It is all you have so put your faith in it.

Summary

The following points should be considered when choosing a psychotherapist.

(1) External qualities: Is the psychotherapist punctual? Does he realize that you are affected by his being late? Does he give adequate warnings for cancellations? In other words does he realize the effect his behaviour has on you? Does he appear to care and be attentive to the task?

(2) Qualifications: Has the therapist had psycho-therapy himself ? How long was he training? Was the training academically rigorous? Has the person been trained to have psychological understanding?

NB. Anyone can stick up a plate and call themselves a psychotherapist. In many countries in the developed world there is no registration of psychotherapists so anyone can legally call himself a psychotherapist. If you called yourself a doctor and started to practise you could be taken to court and punished but if you call yourself a psychotherapist there is no law that can punish you.

More subtle points. Does the therapist spend much of the session time discussing or blaming other people in your life? Does the therapist make interpretations which you agree with but which are also challenging? Does the therapist try to console you or spur you on to change yourself? At the end of a month can you really tell yourself that you have greatly improved. Or have you simply found a sympathetic ear?

GLOSSARY

Cognitive therapy

Form of psychotherapy based on the notion that the way an individual reasons about his or her experiences determines their subsequent behaviour and outlook. The therapist seeks to make patients aware of their negative and distorted thinking and to show them how to substitute more constructive patterns of thinking and behaving.

Counselling

Essentially a relationship between a counsellor and a client in which the counsellor encourages the client to explore his or her thoughts, feelings and behaviour in order to reach a clearer self-understanding and to cope with life more effectively.

Psychiatry

Practice by a medically trained specialist who can diagnose and treat mental disorders. Psychiatric training tends to focus on the biomedical approach to psychological problems and to dispense drugs in treatment.

Psychoanalysis

A term used to describe the theory of development associated with Sigmund Freud and the psychotherapy derived from that theory. Freud maintained that neurotic problems in later life were a product of conflicts that arose during the Oedipal stage of development. These conflicts may have been repressed because the immature ego was unable to cope with them. Psychoanalytic psychotherapy aims to create conditions such that the patient is able to bring these conflicts into consciousness where they can be addressed and dealt with.

Psychology

Most commonly defined as the "scientific study of mind and behaviour". The definition offered by any particular psychologist reflects his or her own interpretative bias, i.e. some would lay more stress on the *mind* part of the definition, others on the *behaviour* part.

Psychotherapy

A general term used to classify treatments for mental disorders in which the treatment is non-physical, such as talking about a problem and modifying behaviour.

BIBLIOGRAPHY

Bloch, S. (1996). *An Introduction to the Psychotherapies* (3rd edn). Oxford, New York: Oxford University Press.

Corey, G. (1985). *The Theory and Practice of Counselling and Psychotherapy* (3rd. edn). Monterey, California: Brooks/Cole Pub. Co.

Dee, G. (1990). *Breaking Through: Making Therapy Succeed for You.* Brudenton, Fla, Human Services Institute, Blue Ridge Summit, PA: Tab Books.

Elliot, A. (1994). *Psychoanalytic Theory. An Introduction.* Oxford, UK & Cambridge, Mass.: Basil Blackwell.

Engler, J., & Goleman, D. (1992). *The Consumer's Guide to Psychotherapy* (with a chapter on psychiatric medicine by Eliot Gelman). New York: Simon & Schuster.

Howe, D. (1993). *On Being a Client: Understanding the Process of Counselling and Psychotherapy.* London: Sage Publications.

Mendelsohn, R. M. (1992). *How Can Talking Help? An Introduction to the Technique of Analytic Therapy.* Northvale, NJ: J. Aronson.

Mitchell, S. A. (1995). *Freud and Beyond. A History of Modern Psychoanalytic Thought.* New York: Basic Books.

Symington, N. (1986). *The Analytic Experience: Lectures From the Tavistock.* London: Free Association.

Tried, E. (1980). *The Courage to Change: From Insight to Self-Innovation.* New York: Brunner/Mazel.

Woodward, J. (1988). *Understanding Ourselves: The Uses of Therapy.* Basingstoke: MacMillan Education.